Published by Evans Brothers Limited
2A Portman Mansions
Chiltern Street
London W1U 6NR

© Evans Brothers Limited 2004

First published 2004

Printed in China

British Library Cataloguing in Publication data.

Powell, Jillian
Jordan has a hearing loss. - (Like Me, Like You)
1. Hearing disorders - Juvenile literature 2. Hearing impaired children - Juvenile literature
I. Title
618.9'20978

ISBN 023752662X

Acknowledgements

The author and publishers would like to thank the following for their help with this book:

Jordan and Amanda Fey; Kate Easdale and the KEBBA Black Belt Academy and Bowplex, Longwell Green, Bristol.

Thanks also to the National Deaf Children's Society for their help in the preparation of this book.

All photographs by Gareth Boden

Credits

Series Editor: Louise John
Editor: Julia Bird
Designer: Mark Holt
Production: Jenny Mulvanny

DIAMOND ANNIVERSARY
1944 · 2004

NDCS

THE NATIONAL
DEAF CHILDREN'S
SOCIETY

Jordan has a
HEARING LOSS

JILLIAN POWELL

Evans

Hi, my name is Jordan and I have a **hearing loss.** I wear two **hearing aids** to help me hear. The doctors found out I had a hearing loss when I was a baby. I'm used to wearing the hearing aids now.

HEARING LOSS

About one or two children in a thousand are born with a hearing loss. Others can develop hearing loss after a serious illness.

I live at home with Mum and my sister Jessica. I love football and my favourite team is Liverpool. I also like swimming, playing on the computer and riding my bike.

7

I wear my hearing aids all the time. The only time I take them off is when I go to bed, and when I'm having a shower or swimming. This is because I mustn't get them wet.

I like going to the cinema. When I go, I flick a switch on my hearing aids so that I can hear the sound better through the cinema's loop system.

LOOP SYSTEMS

Loop systems help hearing aids make sounds clearer by cutting out background noise.

I use a special alarm clock. I put it under my pillow, and in the morning it shakes to wake me up.

When I wake up, I put my hearing aids on straight away. Then I can hear Mum telling me it's time to get ready for school!

While we're having breakfast, the telephone rings. Mum tells me it's for me. I push a special button on the phone to make it louder. It's my friend Alex, asking if I'm coming to **karate** today.

I go to karate class once a week. It's good fun. I get my karate kit ready, then Mum tells me it's time to go.

Kate is our karate teacher. There are lots of children in our class and some of them have a hearing loss like me. We stand at the front so we can hear and see Kate better and copy what she's doing. This is how we start the class.

Sophie and Maddy have a **profound** hearing loss. They talk and understand by using **sign language.** They use their hands to sign different words and ideas. Their faces help them show what they're saying.

SIGN LANGUAGE

Many people who have a hearing loss use sign language to talk and understand.

Today, Kate wants us to practise our kicks. First she tells us what she wants us to do. Then she tells us again, using sign language so Sophie and Maddy can understand. She tells us to keep our knees up and our toes back.

16

We all take turns to practise our kicks with a partner. I'm practising with Alex.

We play games at karate, too. This is my favourite game. It's called Stuck in the Mud. My team is chasing everyone else. Alex and the girls have blue belts. I have a white belt, because I'm still a beginner.

When we're playing games it can get quite noisy! Sometimes I turn my hearing aids down so it's not so bad. When I do this, my friends let me know what's happening by tapping me on the shoulder and speaking to me clearly.

Then we have a break. Sometimes Sophie and Maddy show us how to say something in sign language. I've learned to sign "My name is Jordan."

FINGERSPELLING

Fingerspelling uses the fingers and hands to stand for different letters of the alphabet.

Today, they're teaching me some of the **fingerspelling** alphabet. I try spelling out my name.

The class is over for another week. Mum's here to pick me up. I want to get home quickly because there's a football match on the television and my favourite team is playing!

When I watch television, I wear a headset which lets me make the sound louder so I can hear better. It works from a box in front of the television. Before I had the headset, the television was sometimes too loud for everyone else.

Mum is ringing my teacher to remind her I'll be a bit late to school tomorrow. I have to go to the hospital to have my hearing test. I have a hearing test twice a year. I have to listen for sounds and play a game to show when I hear something.

I have a **radio aid** to wear in school. It helps me hear my teacher better, even when she's on the other side of the classroom. She wears a **microphone** and when she speaks the sounds are sent to my radio aid, then into my hearing aids.

Some days my hearing is worse than others and it's harder to hear what someone is saying when it's noisy. But I've learned to **lip read** by watching people's mouths when they're speaking.

LIP READING

Lip reading means watching the shape of the lips when someone is talking. It can help someone with a hearing loss to understand the words being spoken.

Having a hearing loss doesn't stop me doing all the things I enjoy, especially my favourite thing – going bowling with my friends!

27

Glossary

Fingerspelling using the fingers and hands to stand for different letters of the alphabet

Hearing aid a small aid worn in or behind the ear that makes sounds louder

Hearing loss when someone finds it difficult to hear some sounds, like Jordan

Karate a Japanese art of self-defence

Lip reading watching the lips to read the words being said

Microphone something you speak into that makes sounds louder

Profound hearing loss when someone finds it difficult to hear many sounds, like Sophie and Maddy

Radio aid an aid worn on the body that sends radio waves that are turned into sound waves

Sign language using the hands, body and face to show words, thoughts and ideas

Index

Further Information

UNITED KINGDOM
The National Deaf Children's Society
Tel: 0808 800 8880 (voice and text)
www.ndcs.org.uk
The only UK charity solely dedicated to the support of all deaf children, young deaf people, their parents, carers, families and professionals working on their behalf. NDCS provides balanced information about all aspects of childhood deafness, including education, health, welfare benefits and technology.

Royal National Institute for the Deaf
Tel: 0808 808 0123
www.rnid.org.uk
Information, help and training for deaf people.

British Deaf Association
Tel: 020 7588 3520
www.bda.org.uk
Information and instruction in sign language

UNITED STATES OF AMERICA
American Society for Deaf Children
Tel: 1800 942 2732
www.deafchildren.org
Support and information for families raising children who are deaf or hard of hearing.

AUSTRALIA
The Australian Association of the Deaf
Tel: (02) 9871 8400
www.aad.org.au
Advice and support for deaf people.

NEW ZEALAND
Hearing Association Inc.
Tel: (09) 410 1479
www.hearing.org.nz
Education and resources for people with a hearing loss.

BOOKS
I can't hear like you (Talking it Through), Althea, Happy Cat Books Ltd 2001

My Friend is Deaf, Anna Levene, Chrysalis Children's Books 2003

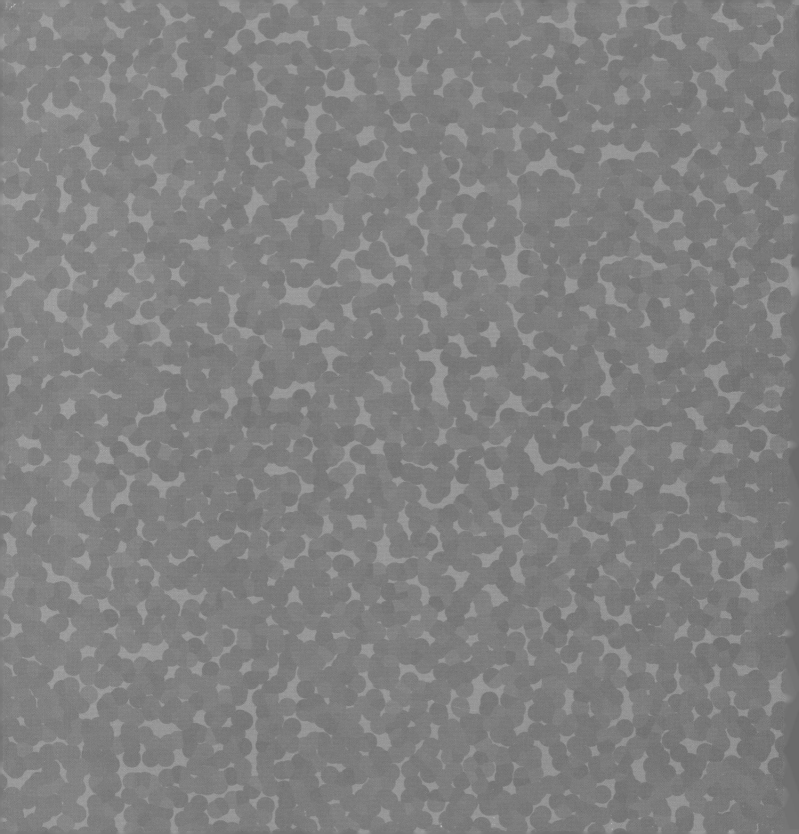